Between The Dark
and The Light

Between The Dark and The Light

R. William Parmenter

Book Cover by R. William Parmenter

Paperback ISBN-13: 979-8-9919836-2-4

eBook ISBN-13: 979-8-9919836-1-7

2nd edition 2024

Content Guidance

This collection contains themes of mental illness, miscarriage, grief, loss, systemic racism, police brutality, and mentions of trauma and suicide.

If you are experiencing suicidal thoughts, please seek help.

For all who bear unseen burdens and bravely endure each day. May words offer you solace, reminding you that you're not alone and may you find your light in the darkness.

Table of Contents

Preface

Dear Reader,

This is a collection created over many years. Poetry has been a part of my life for as long as I can remember. The poems here are mostly from my adult life when I realized that writing was a great outlet for me and my mental health. While not necessarily a replacement for professional therapy, it has helped me process my thoughts and emotions.

In my early teens, the doctors diagnosed me with generalized anxiety disorder, ADHD, and manic depression. Quite a fun mix to experience in the trying times that are the teenage years! Later, as an adult, doctors diagnosed me again with generalized anxiety disorder and ADHD, but now with bipolar disorder, as that is the updated term for manic depression. At the time of this writing, I suspect I may be Autistic. But without a formal evaluation, I hesitate to apply that diagnosis to myself.

I mention all of this, not as some sort of pedigree or qualification, but to connect with others struggling with their mental health, and with those who may have had a similar experience in life. I want to show that it is okay to talk about these experiences as long as it is safe for you to do so. It is okay to know that these mental illnesses are a part of you. While they need not define you, they are how you experience life, and that it is okay to not be okay.

I don't expect this to be read in one sitting. It can get overwhelmingly heavy. Take time with it. Read one or two a day and sit with them for a while. Not all of the poems are about mental health. Some are about life, others about death and mourning. Some are social commentaries that I felt needed to be included because things happening in our societies very much affect us all. Especially if you are the victim of injustices caused by other people, religions, and governments.

Please seek help if you are experiencing suicidal thoughts and hardship. There are many mental health and crisis resources, as well as anonymous hotlines available that are free. Wherever you are, please use them, seek professional help, or reach out to a loved one you trust.

You are not a burden. You are loved. You are valid. You matter.

There is always another word, another sentence, another chapter in your story. Continue writing it; it'll be worth it.

Thank you sincerely for reading this book.

With love,
R. William Parmenter

R. William Parmenter

The Dark

Like curtains drawn
the light dies out—
darkness grows,
and I'm shuttered in.

I can't stop it—
no more than I can stop
my heart from beating
or my lungs from breathing.

Deep in darkened disinterest—
where the seams of life fray,
and where my existence
no longer wants to stay.

Season 41, Episode 8: Dissociation

I float the world,
always the same distance—
ground to eyes,
eyes to sky—
a passive subsistence.

Days blur and feelings mute,
like watching a series—
drifting through episodes,
guessing the finale—
waiting for a twist in the script.

R. William Parmenter

Treading Water

Barely above the surface—
my face just above lapping waves,
and that's on the good days.

At times I slowly sink,
floating deeper through darkened depths—
but never too far, only just.

After a time, I rise
back toward light and air—
my head breaks through, gasping.

I tread to stay afloat,
as the stubborn surly tides
begin pulling me back under.

Unwelcome Guest

It arrives unannounced—
a phantom light,
missing words on the page,
like white out,
with a sudden rage.

Shattered stained glass,
throbbing pain,
right brain bulging,
screaming, pumping vein.

Vision half gone,
body lurching shakes,
open mouth heaves,
my mind in violent quakes.

To my bed, I'm chained,
sweat-drenched sheets,
death feels very near,
its bony fingers reach.

Then it leaves—
a day or two later,
bored of me, gone to hell—
hangover recovery,
my body a hollow shell.

Marathon

Suddenly it hits—
the desire to be done, to quit.
Everything aches, burns;
eyes strain,
holding back tears.

Can I go on?
Do I drag myself
toward the finish?
Or do I stop,
lay down and close my eyes?

A quick glance back—
I see the miles I never thought I'd cross,
and the lengths I've gone to live.

Resolved to continue on—
I ignore the cramps,
the sweating strains of life.
I keep moving—
but I'm so tired,
so very tired.

More Mountains

There are always more mountains—
their sun glanced peaks rise,
looming from a far future horizon.

The cloud-hidden ranges of the past
fade into memory—
those struggles seem so far behind.

Between all the ups and further on downs
there have been valleys of constant growth,
but stagnant swamps and complacent plains
try to hinder my journey forth.

There's always more work to do.

So I plant an unsteady foot,
and reach up with a bruised, tired hand,
to continue up this mountain I climb.

Dust Bunnies

All these little moments in time,
like dust specks in the sun—
blink and miss
a glistening memory.
Then thirty years on
some sound, some word,
some fleeting thought,
coats the present with the past.
That long-forgotten moment—
the one that seemed so important—
just dust, drifting back into the light.

Embarrassed

It faltered, unformed
on the tip of my tongue—
silent spittle slipped
from my lips,
landed squarely
on your shirt,
just above your heart.

Post-Consumer Byproducts

We are made from recycled bits
of generational trauma,
passed down and regurgitated,
but made anew
with the intention to carry on.

Oh, how we strive to break free—
to shed old scabs,
cover the screaming blemishes,
that blur the lines
between abused and abuser.

The healing—
even under band-aids layers—
still leave the scars
of painful memories,
self-inflicted and otherwise.

Social Feed

Endlessly
Scrolling
The feed,
Searching
For life's
Answers,
Trading
Likes
For worth—
As if
The opinions
Of strangers
Could ever
Fill the void.

Unboxing

They try to fit us in
these prepackaged boxes,
labeled by someone else's
ideals of function
and form.

But we don't fit.

So they try extra tape—
covering our mouths,
binding hands,
bowing heads.

But they forget—

We can stretch,
tear off their weak tape,
shred their simple boxes,
and toss their judgments
straight to the dumpster.

Bullied

I'll never forget that summer
he tied me to a tree
and ate my bowl of Frosted Flakes
right in front of me.

Or all the times he shoved
a large filthy finger
into my peanut butter and jelly—
a dark, oozing hole left in my anger.

Or the times he forced me
to pound fizzy, cold beers
with the threat of his fist—
I was overcome with preteen fear.

Then there's that other guy
who punched me after gym
my head ached as he spewed
hatred for a lie shared with him.

And that other angry dude
my bumper stickers he didn't like,
he honked and he harassed,
tried to force me to fight.

I often wonder
if they've ever found help.

'Merica

Here,
where fistfuls of mud
are flung onto the face
of the different.

Here,
with hands wiped clean,
they now blame the different
for the puddles.

Wake Up

Anxiety's up
humanity's down—
our Black neighbors pushed around.
Chastised, choked, and choking
their heads held to the ground.

"I can't breathe," he cries.
We gasp, point fingers—
filming from a distance.
"Please help," they scream.
We hem and haw, complicit in silence.

The cop's reaper verdict
kills so easily—
while stupefied bystanders
cling tight
to white fragility.

Their precious pearls clutched
between silky shaken hands—
empty thoughts and prayers
fall upon quiet lips, as
"all lives matter," scream the deniers.

But as peaceful people march for change?
"Armed, looting thugs," we're told.
Yet, trigger-twitchy white boys
storm capitols with a free pass.
"Very fine people" we're sold.

Years of oppression,
met with raised fists
against systemic suppression;
watching on the sidelines,
frustration fires now burn.

So, the streets are now filled
with broken glass and burning buildings—
in teargas fog the innocents scatter,
while commanders-in-chief
fan the flames and hold the hammer.

Loss Of Cognition

Human condition,
loss of cognition—
no love, no empathy
no compassion.

Wanton greed,
power lust,
war and genocide—
man's only must.

Will we ever see
a time of consistent peace,
where all can be
and simply exist?

Or will we rage on,
throwing stones, stabbing sticks,
until there's nothing
but oceans of bone and plastic?

Writer's Block

I'm haunted by stories—
ghostly visages in my head,
their nameless voices clouding
my unquiet brain.

They demand to be let out—
locked in their conscience prison.
There's a key,
but I lost it.

Imperfection

Startled face,
shaggy hair,
bushy brows all a mess.
I'm gangly, lengthy
clothes all wrinkled and stressed.

Tongue-tied talking
my voice is too deep.
Explains nothing to no one,
overthinking creep.

My poems hardly rhyme
my writings a sham.
My drawings? No good.
Ideas? Bland.

Perfections no joke—
I can't, I can't...
Yet I try, and I try
again and again,
and again.

R. William Parmenter

The   Bed   Stays Unmade

Weakened and shadow cast,
my worn out mind sleeps in.
Comforters provide little
as they're corner crumpled—
my hands to my face
with wrinkled sheets—
I'm pillowed in darkness.
Though subtle light creeps in
from behind shaded windows,
I'm blind to the constant world.
Not a caring eye goes
to the floor piled clothes
hampering the daily dress rehearsal.
So the bed stays unmade
while I slumber the day,
refusing to join the hustle.

Fragile

My porcelain confidence
balances at the edge of doubt.
One careless bump let's down my guard
sends it all crashing down,
I'm shattered into a million shards.

Blankets

Inside I slide
under the weight
of a blanket womb.
It's comforting embrace
A refuge from a violent world—
Keeping me safe
From the monsters below.

Arguments With Myself

Fictitious arguments
scream in my head
with ghosts of the past
and new ones for the future.

They crowd my brain
with angry rants
and retorts
that spiral nowhere.

These voices mire
any semblance of rest—
yet I argue on
with no one but myself.

Reforged

Fiery thoughts burn fierce,
full of painful memories.
Take and melt them down
to a basic, liquid form.

Cast me from the crucible,
into a mold for a blade—
let it cool
dull, rough, and unmade.

Stick me back in the fire—
let rage set me ablaze,
then hammer me on the anvil
drawing out fear, doubt, and shame.

As I take shape,
throw me in a steaming vat—
quench to a hardened resolve—
now sharp, useful, and true.

Insomnia

I suffer for sleep,
panic paralyzed,
screaming inside—
midnight shapes
shift and swirl
in my full moon mind.

Fractal beams of light—
and the eyelid cinema—
flash fractured thoughts,
while tinnitus screams
a shrilling shriek
twisting me in a thousand knots.

Frustrated limbs
flail to find
the perfect comforting spots—
grant me endless sleep,
take my soul to keep,
I beg the sleeping gods.

Emma Jean

There was a seed
that started to sprout,
planted in a loving pot—
watered with hopes and dreams.

Too soon, you withered—
stolen by cruel winds,
never to grow above the soil.
Our hearts shattered.

We wrestle with the what-ifs,
the whys that echo endlessly,
seeking meaning,
trying to accept.

Like a landlocked storm,
sadness saturated us—
for what happened,
for what could've been.

And yet, your spirit blooms within us,
a blossom upon our hearts—
a gentle reminder,
of life's fragility.

Flowers for the Tide

A low tide stroll
overcast gray—
the steady waves roared,
rumbled toward the shore.

A white rose tumbled adrift,
beaching upon the sand,
as if searching for new shores
to plant its roots.

Another rose drifted near,
then another—
dots of white petals
bobbed gently afloat.

They pointed the way,
like lights along a road,
leading toward a lost soul
taken by the sea.

R. William Parmenter

The Shadow Behind

I sense it—
that shadow behind,
its clammy hands
reaching for my neck.

It's always there,
like a film noir,
replaying slowly
a silent horror.

It'll grasp,
and I'll gasp—
until the world blurs
fading to black.

Seasonal Affective

I'm the winter solstice,
cold and unforgiving,
where darkness reigns.

I'm the spring equinox,
when light grows,
and flowers bloom.

I'm the summer solstice
whose warmth sings,
a radiant crescendo.

I'm the autumn equinox,
shedding a gown full of color,
before winter's naked cold returns.

R. William Parmenter

Mourning
Childhood

I still mourn
the death of my childhood.

I mourn
under that deep blue sky—
the grinding groan of airplanes overhead—
boats, I'd pretend,
sailing over me.
Great tall trees of seaweed,
bird fish,
and my bike, a submarine.

I mourn
those long hours, summer days,
barefoot in cool grass,
collecting the world.
watching ants, mandible and 'tenna,
fight like school bullies—
I so dreaded to return.

I mourn
the clink clank of kitchen sounds,
meaty onion sizzled dinner smells,
while robins sang their evening song—
as the setting sun settled
through an open curtain window.

I mourn
the innocence and wonder

of the faraway moon,
and magic hidden behind those stars—
as fireflies danced and flashed
to rhythmic cricket song.
Sheets tucked, a forehead kiss,
and eyes drifted into careless dreams.

How quickly I buried it all
not knowing how long I'd mourn.

R. William Parmenter

Mirror

I stare at this haggard person
in the long-set mirror,
not sure who it is anymore.
I mean, it is me—
who else could they be?

I blink, they blink.
We tilt our heads questioningly.
Our mouths open, then close.
We do not speak—
our tongues lash out in raspberries,
but the laughter never comes.

Our dark-set eyes squint
disappointed with one another,
we turn from ourselves,
leaving each other.

Little Blue Pill

The doctor gave me
a little blue pill—
said it would make me
feel more real.

I think it's working,
holding back the shadows,
but the darkness still watches,
lying quiet, lurking low.

Is this pill my flashlight
in the dark?
Will it change me,
free me?
Will it pull me up
from those twisted caverns
that led me so far down?

R. William Parmenter

Between The Dark and The Light

Twilight thoughts linger
beneath heavy-lidded eyes,
rising with the dawning day.
I lie in silent solitude,
contemplating what was
and what could be.

A fleeting calm
before depressive clouds gather,
with their dark, growling bellows
that mire the mind
with foggy doubt
and anxious undertows.

Or will a manic whirlwind
swirl in hurricane gusts,
To fill my slackened sails—
sending this chaos craft
on a breathless, lightning odyssey
lost in restless gales.

It is in this moment—
between the dark and the light—
for now I find a solace home.
But the sun begins to swell,
lifting night's gentle veil,
revealing who I'll become.

Happy, For Once

I float like dandelion fuzz
on a whirling wind—
a wish blown free,
gliding gently along.

I feel reborn—
laughing genuinely,
loving fully,
living presently.

I want to cling to this,
though I know I'll land—
grounded for a time
in the still darkness.

Such is life—
it, too, will pass.
And when the wind returns,
I'll float once more.

Lint

I'm running regrets
and churning choices
of shoulda', coulda', woulda',
instead of accepting—
it is what it is.

Decisions were made
in manic moments
of striding panic,
the best of intentions—
I now sit with them.

Scars and monetary regression
leave me empty,
like these pockets—
only lint left
to soften the shame.

Panic

Like scuttling cockroaches,
it skitters up from dark corners—
those cobwebbed old habits
inside of me.

My heart pumps quickly,
as if I'm running
from the hungry animals
of life's endless demands.

Part fear — part excitement,
like stepping on stage
to sing of subtle rage
for the very first time.

My fingers bleed
as I pick and bite,
wrangling this creature
striving for control.

Focus on deep breathing...
Inhale.
Exhale.
Calm.
Calm...
Calm.

Drowning

I've fallen from my vessel
into a sea of people.
Their bacterial hands
grasp and grab,
grope and wave.

Twitch and shiver—
my skin squirms.
Their invasive eyes
watching, judging.

I scream—
but silenced
by their droning drink of voices.
My heart bludgeoning beats
and my broken breath bleeds.

I reach for anything
as fear floods over.
No escape,
I resign,
slowly slipping under—

down,
and
down,
and
down.

A Minute

Sometimes,
take a minute
from the strife
of modern life.

Breathe,
let the mind play—
watch the undulating rhythm
of leaves in the trees,
gently dancing on the breeze.

Listen to the hum of bees
bounce from
honey-scented flowers,
their tiny legs laden—
luggage filled with pollen.

Gaze from the grass
up at bulbous white clouds—
make up shapes,
a fluffy cat, roaring dragons,
or castles made of cakes.

Only a minute to pause—
to remember how precious life is.

Summer Dreams

There was a time
I'd fall asleep
with the window open—
the cool night air
breaking the summer sweat.
Crickets chirped,
while distant trains
wailed warnings into the night.

Often, I'd imagine
drifting through the window,
to commune with twilight spirits.
We'd gather at the station
before the final call,
then tip our hats and bid farewell,
boarding the moonlit train
bound for the stars.

Back to Nature

Time to sit with a forest,
and commune with the trees—
hear their sylvan whispers
calming me with ease.

Ground in the soil,
dig roots deep and free—
let go of old burdens
that no longer serve me.

I'll reach to the sky,
my branches up high—
breathing in new life
in the sun's giving light.

I'll toughen my bark,
growing steady within—
adding layers of wisdom,
to stand tall against the wind.

Being Human

We are human—
masculine, feminine, nonbinary
a fluid spectrum—
all parts of a whole,
but individuals in our expression.

We are human—
The sun, the moon
Earth, stars, galaxy,
elemental flow,
universal energy.

We are human—
past and present,
memories and losses,
ancestor ashes,
specters of progress.

We are human—
creative, destructive
flesh and bone,
ideas and failures,
thoughts, our own.

We are human—
flawed but learning,
seeking, growing—
a paradoxical existence,
always becoming.

All For What?

We live—
faster and faster,
burning that oil, turning those wheels,
making those dollars,
putting in hours
for greedy corporate shares.

All for what?

We fight—
teeth gnashing, cyber bashing,
them, not us. You, not me.
Majorities gather en masse—
bullets, bombs, and slurs—
thrown at the underserved.

All for what?

We exploit—
Earth and Her glory,
animal, mineral, all up for grabs.
The praise of power—
take it, own it—
their lives colonized.

All for what?

We die—
one and the same,
peasant and king,

candles without flame.
No matter what we possess,
we are only whispers in dust and ash.

All for what?

Toxic Positivity

Like radioactive waste,
plastic smiling
can cause harm.

Moth

Warm and safe
wrapped around myself,
I felt protected
from the cold, cruel world.

But something stirred
within—
I needed a change.

Wriggling free those old, tired ways,
shredding the silk of trauma—
a cocoon of withdrawal falling.

My wings, once frail,
now stretch wide in the light—
I prepare to take flight.

Cut From Different Cloth

Cut from different cloth—
not entirely straight,
with anxious angles
and procrastinated patterns.

It's woven with shadow,
yet streaked with light—
expected to endure—
yet too soft for this world.

But I'm learning to love it—
it's beautiful—
it's me.

Sudden Ending

It could come anytime, you know—
the crash of a car,
a fall down the stairs,
the creeping encroachment of cancers.

It could be unexpected, you know—
a meteor crash,
the rising climactic seas,
or a burning nuclear flash.

I'd prefer it quick and sudden; you know—
asleep in bed,
closed eyes, no warning.
The end.

Just Give Me A Reason

Waiting breath bated
for the next tragedy
to give the anxiety
an excuse to cling to.

R. William Parmenter

Broken Parts

Broken parts from a bin
a piecemeal shamble
held together by thin
hopes and dreams.

Fragile threads unravel,
Pieces slip away—
remove the rubble,
and rusted remains.

New parts are found,
welded good and strong.
To be made whole,
ready to move on.

Shape those plans,
embrace the change—
falling apart doesn't mean
the decay of distant dreams.

Callous Grit

I grew up in a place
where calloused hands
measured your worth.

The most hours on the clock
crowned you the working-class king—
punch in,
punch out.

But if you're soft,
throw in the towel.
No time for sissies—
stop whining, get moving.

Grab that shovel,
pick up that hammer—
dig your grave
nail your coffin.

R. William Parmenter

Joy Ride

I am a rusted old heap—
a rickety car with an outdated map.

How I've dragged us
up hills and down steep grades,
through missteps, meanderings,
and reckless wrong turns.

You, the ever-patient mechanic,
keeping me on course—
guiding and mending—
a steady hand on the wheel.

And here we are now,
the odometer turning over—
joy riding life's winding roads,
completely clutched in love.

Fledglings

It's as if
we're waiting
for our parents' generation
to die—
before shedding our shells.

It's as if
we still seek
their elusive approval—
a final nod—
to grow our wings.

It's as if
we're afraid of flying,
afraid of our own feathers,
or the wind,
or time.

It's as if
we're waiting
for the next big disaster—
a diagnosis, a death—
before taking the leap.

It's as if
we're too tethered
to the familiar and same,
never to soar
into the unknown.

Introvert

Withdrawn, they call me,
but very much aware.
Quiet, reserved
as the talkers
wag their chins.

Watching, waiting
for an opening
to slip in a thought
or witty remark.

But as always,
the moment's passed.

In The Coffee Aisle
One Afternoon

I saw someone I used to know
but I was too shy to say hello.
I browsed bags of coffee beans,
as they scanned the shelves looking for things.

I wanted to avoid social awkwardness—
the forgetting of names and knowing less,
or stumbling over those right things to say—
What's up, how's it goin', having a good day?

The who's, the why's, and whenever when's
the complicated how ya been—
like choosing between the best bean blend —
I stayed in place instead.

Finally, I found a favorite light roast,
the smooth, nutty flavor I like most,
then turned and saw them go idly by;
maybe next time I'll have the courage to say hi.

Anyway, it was good to see you.

Growing Old

Another day dawns
Through the crack
Of sleep-deprived eyes
Arthritic aches rising—
Stretch to move.

Change jingling
In a threadbare pocket,
While the shore offers more stones
And wrinkles, like waves.

Cling to the ghosts
Of old friends and lovers,
As time slips through
Bony fingers like sand—
Castles washed away with the tide.

Late-night contemplation
As the moon fades on the horizon—
With a last promise unmet,
Only the universe remains
To offer an endless embrace.

Men Don't Cry

Do my best—
the good partner,
the good father,
employee of the month.

Creator, provider, human—
is it ever enough?
Future faulting failures
quake my existence.

Driven drained, defeated—
near the brink of tears—
a man, they say,
should never cry.

So, my eyes stay dry.

Manic Projects

Do all the things—
Learn to write,
Learn to code,
Learn to play
Violin, piano, drums, and ukulele.

Vocal lessons, cooking sessions,
Graphic design, illustrations,
Gaming, gardening, photography,
Painting, and crochet.
Don't forget the reading foray.

Jump first, think after,
Not enough time,
Faster, faster, faster.

Everything started,
Nothing sustained,
Crashing down,
Fun drowned out
By the ever-living strain.

Grasping For Strings

I'm grasping for strings
attached to dreams
floating through endless skies.

Wandering ideas
wild on the wind,
I catch one and hold it a while.

Another drifts nearby,
its color bright as fire—
I grab that one, too.

Then a third appears,
and another, and another,
but my hands are full.
So, I sadly watch them drift away,
and wonder what might have been.

R. William Parmenter

Turntable

I'm broken
I'm broken
I'm broken
I'm broken
I'm broken I'm broken
I'm
Broken.

Fix the stylus
Let it glide smoothly through the grooves.
Vibrations align
Harmonize harmoniously
And my music sings again.

And again,
And again,
And again,
And again,
And again.

Cast The Compass

Cast the compass
over a cliff.
Get lost in living.
Forget the days,
drift through aimless hours.

Meander through moments,
and savor the destinations—
a journey with no map—
where time is marked by sunsets,
leaving only the now to wander.

Mortality

My flame burns
bright as the morning sun—
fresh upon the wick.

As the day passes,
I socially melt—
waning wax drips.

Responsibilities taper
my tall resolve
shrinking to snubbed confidence.

By night I'm dim—
my fickle flame falters—
snuffed to a wisp in darkness.

Poetry and a Dog

Poetry and a dog saved my life—
my finger on the trigger
as my golden dog scratched open the door,
her head upon my knee, whimpering
as I shuddered to cry.
Tears fell to the floor
like the clinking of unloaded bullets.
I picked them up to load my pen,
and wrote my mind upon the page—
the words of a bleeding heart.

R. William Parmenter

Unfinished

I tried to end it a few times;
that cold pull of the trigger,
a gulp of little pills—
my toes on the infinite edge.

Plans made, postponed;
for now, I've chosen to live,
I've chosen to thrive—
there's always another time.

A letter unfinished;
I'm writing a new chapter,
the lonely cursor blinks,
waiting for what comes next.

Box Of Photos

We're only here for a moment—
a quick camera click
of forgotten photos,
bundled in a dusty box—
Polaroids of better times
nestled with the faded receipts
of failures and regrets.

R. William Parmenter

To Create

When writing or drawing
I am alive—
in the present—
painting with words or brush.

Ensconced and enlivened,
a flurry of creation—
the world forgotten—
in a fever rush.

My mind a whirlwind,
ideas abound—
I strive to stay with—
this mad creative bout.

I do what I can
an inspired race against time—
as the end looms near—
when the will is murdered by doubt.

Wildflowers

Like wildflowers,
they bloom into our lives—
a passion of color and life—
we breathe in their love.

In a season too brief, they pass—
as nature's wheel turns—
their memories forever held,
pressed between the pages of our heart.

The Light

That moment—
when it's decided
to throw open the dusty curtains,
letting golden light flood
this darkened, stuffy room—
is miraculous.

A contented sigh, a rare smile—
goose bumps rising on parched skin
as creaking bones stretch high,
and a sighing breath
clears the stagnated air
of a once shuttered mind.

That moment—
when life is fresh as air,
and all is ready and waiting
like a pause between heartbeats—
grasp it and go.
Claim your light.

Acknowledgments

Monica, saying thanks on this page doesn't cover the immense love and gratitude I have for you each and every day. Your guidance and patience with this broken mess of a husband is nothing short of amazing. Thank you for your constant encouragement to follow my dreams.

To Krystal N. Craiker, thank you so much for your encouragement and inspiration to continue to write. It is an honor to be able to watch you write and publish great stories, achieving your dreams.

Jaime Dill, of Polish & Pitch, I cannot thank you enough for looking at this work, providing input, and giving me the confidence to push forward and publish. Without you, this collection would still be in a cluttered folder on a tired, old hard-drive.

To my friends and family, who continue to inspire and strive for the best in yourselves; I thank you.

About The Author

R. William Parmenter was born and raised in Michigan. There, his love of writing prose and poetry cultivated, especially when the weeds of mental illness took root. As an adult, he lived and traveled around Arizona, California, Oregon, and Washington, where a love of the Pacific Northwest grew. However, his heart lies in Michigan, where he's returned to write, create art, and explore with his family.

www.ingramcontent.com/pod-product-compliance
Lightning Source LLC
Chambersburg PA
CBHW030510130626
46549CB00007B/2921